It's about time

Jack Beers

Longman

Edinburgh Gate
Harlow, Essex

The small hand
on a clock is called
the hour hand.
The hour hand
is pointing to the 7.
It means the time is
about seven o'clock.

Kelly
wakes up.

Ling-Ling
wakes up.

The big hand
on a clock is called
the minute hand.
It is pointing
straight up.
It means the time is
exactly seven o'clock.

Ling-Ling and Kelly eat breakfast.

The hour hand is between the 7 and the 8.
It is halfway between the 7 and the 8.
It means the time is about half past seven.

The minute hand points straight down.
It means that the time is exactly half past seven.

Ling–Ling and Kelly say goodbye to Mum.

The hour hand is pointing close to the 9. It points just before the 9. It means the time is just before nine o'clock.

Ling-Ling watches Kelly go to her classroom.

The hour hand
is pointing
close to the 9.
It points
just past the 9.
It means the time
is just past
nine o'clock.

The hour hand is pointing halfway between the 9 and the 10. What time is it now?

Ling-Ling's class listens to Mrs Chin read from a book.

The minute hand
is pointing
straight down.
What time is it
now?

Ling-Ling and her class enjoy a game.

Ling-Ling and Kelly eat together.

Lunch starts at twelve o'clock.
Is it lunch time yet?
How can you tell?

Ling-Ling is in her maths lesson.

Is it half past twelve?
Or is it half past one?

Ling-Ling's favourite lesson is Chinese.

Chinese class starts
at one o'clock.
Has the lesson started yet?

Kelly is practising for a play.

School ends at three o'clock.
Is it time to go home yet?

Goodbye, Ling-Ling.
Goodbye, Kelly.